YOUR ASSERTIVE LIFE SERIES

ATTITUDE
ADVANTAGE

Andy Raingold

YOUR ASSERTIVE LIFE SERIES

ATTITUDE ADVANTAGE

Simple Steps to Elevate Yourself and Your Life by Becoming Your Own Best Friend, Once and for All!

Written By:
Andy Raingold

Graphic Design By: Stephen Hawkins.
Special Thanks to Nathanial Dasco & Ikhide Oshoma

Your Assertive Life Series Copyright 2020 ThinkeLife

All Rights Reserved.
No part of this book may be reproduced in any form or by any electronic or mechanical means including information storage and retrieval means without permission in writing from the author.

The only exception is by a reviewer, who may quote short excerpts in a review.

Andy Raingold - ThinkeLife
Visit my website at **www.andyraingold.com**

First printing: Sept 2020.

ISBN: 978 1 913929 30 5

Table of Contents

INTRODUCTION 1

THE ATTITUDE ADVANTAGE 1

PART 1: CHANGE YOUR ATTITUDE - CHANGE YOUR LIFE 3

    THE MEANING OF ATTITUDE 4
    DOES ATTITUDE REALLY MATTER? 4
    THE IMPORTANCE OF ATTITUDE 5
    IS ATTITUDE EVERYTHING? 6
    THE MOST IMPORTANT SUCCESS ATTITUDES 7
    ATTITUDE AND FINANCES 10
    "NEVER GIVE UP" ALWAYS HELPFUL ATTITUDE 10
    HOW DO I CHANGE MY ATTITUDE? 12

THE POSITIVE ATTITUDE 13

    POSITIVE VS NEGATIVE ATTITUDES 13
    HOW TO CULTIVATE A POSITIVE ATTITUDE? 14
    ENCOURAGING A POSITIVE ATTITUDE IN OTHERS 16
    POSITIVE THINKING AND DAILY ROUTINES 17
    FACING YOUR FEARS 19
    ATTITUDE BEGINS WITH SELF-AWARENESS 20

PART 2: GETTING YOUR ATTITUDE ON YOUR SIDE 21

PART 3: MAKE YOUR ATTITUDE YOUR VERY BEST FRIEND! 22

WHAT DOES IT MEAN TO GET YOUR ATTITUDE ON YOUR SIDE? 23

DIFFERENT WAYS TO GET YOUR ATTITUDE ON YOUR SIDE 26

DEFINITION OF A POSITIVE ATTITUDE 29

POSITIVE LIVING TIPS 30

YOUR NEW BEST FRIEND 33

USING YOUR ATTITUDE AS YOUR BEST FRIEND 34

WHAT MAKING YOUR ATTITUDE YOUR FRIEND CAN DO FOR YOU? 38

AN EXAMPLE OF MAKING YOUR ATTITUDE YOUR FRIEND 41

SUMMING IT UP 45

OTHER BOOKS BY ANDY RAINGOLD 50

Introduction

The Attitude Advantage

The Attitude Advantage is a simple method to get your attitude on your side to achieve even better results than you are getting right now. It's that simple.

I'm really excited to help you *Elevate Your Attitude* through the Attitude Advantage and to start getting even more out of life than you are right now.

I can't think of anything more worthwhile than to begin right away to elevate your current attitude in order to take advantage of your attitude in every area of life and to begin to get more out of everything you do and every experience you have within each area of your life.

From this point forward we will refer to the Attitude Advantage as an effect of Elevating your Attitude and how that can have both subtle and profound effects on the results you get in just about every area of your life. if you want to succeed more in your job, career, or business then this little book *"Attitude Advantage - Simple Steps to Elevate Yourself and Your Life by Becoming Your Own Best Friend, Once and for All!"* can help you to do so over the short and long term. And, if you want to get more out of your relationships then the *Attitude Advantage* can help in that area too.

In fact, *Attitude Advantage* can help you to improve just about every area of your life that's possible to improve. All it takes is a little thought and effort to take your first steps to elevate yourself and your life.

But Be Warned: Elevating Your Attitude through the Attitude Advantage takes constant ongoing effort... There are no easy fixes or shortcuts. You have to put in the effort to get the results from these methods just like you have to put effort into just about everything else in life. But the rewards can be great. And that is all determined by the effort you put in, both the quantity and the quality of the effort count towards achieving a better attitude and a better life experience.

Either way, this short guide will set you in the right direction and help you get over any obstacles you may now be facing. So, let's start right at the beginning.

PART 1:
Change Your Attitude - Change Your Life

The Meaning of Attitude

The term *attitude* is being used on a daily basis by most English-speaking people, and often the meaning of the term gets lost in its use. This term has become so popular that common sense dictates that everyone knows how to use it but doesn't exactly know what it is.

The definition of attitude is multi-faceted and generally, it means a person's position towards a subject or topic. In simple terms, an attitude is an emotional or intellectual reaction to a certain subject, behavior, or piece of information. It is the way humans respond to the circumstances of life.

"A feeling or opinion about something or someone, or a way of behaving that is caused by this"- Definition of Attitude by Cambridge Dictionary

Does Attitude Really Matter?

Attitude is a topic and motivational driving force that is often vastly underestimated by people. In fact, often you will hear advice towards life circumstances that disregard it completely. 'Just get on with it' or 'keep pushing and don't think about it too much, comes to mind. However, such advice, when disconnected from the rightly required attitude, can be catastrophic to the success of any endeavor. This is because willpower, without the right attitude, can only take you so far and burnout is far more likely to happen in those who have not yet adopted the right attitude for their life ventures. Our attitude, therefore, is something that is extremely important if you are looking to achieve something greater in this world. I say something greater because wherever you find yourself right now is mostly an effect of the attitudes towards life and others that you have held up until this point.

However, not only in the realm of those chasing success is the changing of attitudes necessary. Life will undoubtedly become difficult at times even if you are happy not building your life out towards something greater than the average person. And the specific circumstances that make it so may be completely outside of your control. Nevertheless, our attitudes will always remain within our sphere of influence, no matter how hard our life may be, and this means that we always retain some level of control and power over our state of being and the results we are getting.

It may be, therefore, not too much to say that attitude not only matters but that it may be one of the most important things in life, whether you want to be successful or simply content with your current lot in life.

The Importance of Attitude

As stated above, the negligence of right attitudes can have dire consequences. However, while there may be some attitudes that are far-reaching and all-encompassing for our lives in general, it is sometimes more important to check our attitudes towards the most important aspects of our lives individually. This is because every person who desires positive change and growth in their personal life will need to take a good look at their attitudes towards meaningful subjects in their personal life, in order to speed up their journey, if only a little.

According to Marine Insight (2019) our attitudes do not just determine some of our actions but in fact all of them. Think about it for a moment, the last time you said something you shouldn't have. Is it because of your attitude towards a certain person? How about when you voted for your favorite politician? Do you remember how you felt towards their policies or character and were those feelings not a great motivating force in your decision?

No matter how objective people may want to be, their attitudes will be a determining factor in the decisions that they make. They become a sort of filter by which we make our decisions and make choices in life.

Now, if someone has the right attitude within a particular area of life, this can mean that they make fruitful decisions that create growth and prosperity in their lives and in the lives of those around them. However, bad attitudes can be toxic and can quickly lead to isolation. Think about it, does anyone really want to spend significant time with someone who complains a lot or someone who has little interest in bettering themselves? And indeed, has little interest in others? Therefore, because attitude influences your actions and your actions in your life, it is inexplicably true that attitude is of very high importance.

Is Attitude Everything?

Before going further into the explanation of the positive aspects of attitude, it is important to take a step back and create a more nuanced and holistic perspective. It is undeniable that attitude is important, for the reasons we have already outlined. However, it cannot be said that attitude is everything. Think about it like a car. If someone was to ask you, what is the most important component of a car you may get multiple answers ranging from the steering wheel to the motor or perhaps even the wheels?

However, the true answer is that without all the necessary components the car will not be able to fulfill its function. Attitude is like one of those car components, like the wheels or the motor. It is undoubtedly necessary for success and happiness in life but it has to be balanced out by other factors such as purpose, self-discipline, willpower, resources, and plans. Without all of these components, when looking at attitude from the angle of achieving success, it is just about impossible to reach your goal. Therefore, do not make the mistake of seeing attitude as the whole car, even though it is one of its most important aspects, much like all of the other components. However much like the wheels of a car make all of the other car functions possible, so does attitude color most aspects of an individual. Usually being applied to each area of life which then culminates in the whole life and a more general outlook or attitude.

The Most Important Success Attitudes

As we start to delve deeper into attitudes, looking at the most important attitudes to have is key. This is in terms of individual subjects as well as the attitude surrounding that subject as these usually color your more general attitude towards others and life in general:

1. A Hopeful and Optimistic Attitude Towards Life

In a world filled with negativity, pain, and suffering it is easy to lose your hope in life and become somewhat pessimistic. When this happens to someone, they can often find themselves becoming extremely cynical despite not being consciously aware of it. According to Psychology Today (2018), cynics are actually often the first to suffer from their own attitudes in life. As they keep from social engagement in the public sphere and often fail to make true contributions to themselves and society, they find themselves quickly becoming outcasts in their communities. A cynic in short believes that there is no point in life and that all things are to be viewed from the worst possible angle.

However, taking a hopeful attitude towards life is far more rewarding to the individual practicing it, as well as those in his/her immediate sphere of influence or environment. This then becomes someone who has a hopeful and optimistic attitude towards life and will generally attempt to see situations for the value they can provide rather than the harm they have done.

By directing their focus to these positive aspects, it becomes almost impossible for the hopeful person not to see that all things, whether originally deemed good or bad, can have a positive impact in one way or another. This attitude will lead to an increase of friends, as people are drawn to people with hopeful and optimistic attitudes, which in turn will then boost your own happiness, as strong social networks have been shown to be one of the primary determining factors in someone's happiness.

2. An Understanding Attitude Towards People

Whether you like it or not humans are a social species and you will have to interact with others in order to stay a functioning member of society. Because of this, it is important to obtain the right attitude towards others, as not doing so can lead to conflict, hostility, and the breakdown of communities. And the most important attitude that one can develop to help the individual with their interactions with others is one of understanding.

Every person on the planet has a personal story filled with experiences that twist and shape their reality, values, and belief systems. However, it is not uncommon for those things to begin clashing with others who do not share the same values or beliefs. When this happens, it can lead to a major communication breakdown, which in the best-case scenario leads to parties being slightly annoyed with one another while in the worst-case scenario it could mean world war. Countless wars can be seen as two distinct ideologies clashing with one another after verbal debate has broken down. Because of the dangers of not understanding someone else's life journey, their beliefs, and values, it is important to always attempt to understand someone else.

So, the next time your colleague says something that annoys you, try to see life through their lens. Maybe they are having marriage problems and are therefore more irritable than usual, or perhaps they have been struggling with a pornography addiction. One of the worst traps you can fall into is to believe that only your life is difficult and hard and that everyone else has it easy. As the author Sherrilyn Kenyon once said:

"Everyone suffers" And because of this fact, you will be able to

avoid conflict as long as you maintain an understanding attitude towards people. Less conflict for you means more time and energy for the things that truly matter.

3. A Humble Attitude Towards Yourself

"When pride comes, then comes disgrace, but with humility comes wisdom"

While being humble may have devolved in certain circles to cheesy one-liners that get plastered onto Instagram stories, it is still one of the most important attitudes to have in life. People often misunderstand what it means to truly be humble and instead practice self-depreciation. However, this is not the true purpose and expression of humility.

Being humble means that you are willing to look at yourself through a truthful lens, to see your flaws, and be honest about them but also to acknowledge your strengths and act with self-respect whenever the situation demands it.

However, human beings have great difficulty with being truly humble, as things like the 'humble brag' where someone may post a picture or video on social media that just so happens to show off their new sports car, is becoming all the more the norm.

However, a lack of humility is nothing new but it is often said that the most successful people are also the humblest. That is because when you decide to be prideful, which basically means you deceive yourself about who you are, you are priming yourself for a superiority complex, deteriorating your relationships, and taking on tasks or responsibilities you do not have the ability to handle or in some cases afford. Confidence is good and often we need to believe that we can step outside of our comfort zone and accomplish a thing, but the need for humility to balance that confidence is key in order to become the best version of yourself and to create success in your life and those around you.

Attitude And Finances

Unbeknownst to many, your attitude can have a direct impact on your finances, whether that be positive or negative. The famous book "Think and Grow Rich" by Napoleon Hill outlines this concept beautifully by explaining how our mindset is what stops us from becoming financially successful. Someone who is in a "poverty" mindset for example will rarely act on his finances the same way that someone who has a "prosperity" mindset. The former will tend to buy things that they do not need, such as large televisions, the best mobile phone, or expensive designer clothes. The latter however will often opt for cheaper alternatives such as local supermarket clothes and a second-hand car and use the money that they save to either invest in their future or save for a greater investment later.

The difference between the two could be hard to see from an outside perspective, they may both have a family, both work similar earning jobs and both have comparable skill sets. However, it is likely that if you were to follow their journey over the years that the person who suffers from a poverty mindset will continue to make decisions that will support that position. Medium (2018) defines the poverty mindset as being based on scarcity, as they do not believe there is enough money, they do not use the money they do have to invest in themselves. However, the person who has adopted an attitude of prosperity will not be afraid to make those investments. And while some of them will not amount to much, some will grow and prosper, leading to greater financial affluence. Therefore, having the right attitude when it comes to your finances is crucial if you want to have a successful financial life.

"Never Give Up" Always Helpful Attitude

Many within the personal development and self-help community have taken the old advice of "never give up" and put it on steroids. This unfortunate perversion of the underlying truth is why so many people who are trying to become successful and better their lives are failing. They do not understand the subtle nuance: never give up on being successful and happy, but sometimes you will have to change the route by which you are trying to achieve that goal. Seth Godin goes into this phenomenon very deeply in his book titles, The Dip.

And that is what makes all the difference when discussing the never-give-up attitude, you have to know exactly where it is helpful and where it is destructive. Take, for example, John. John is a young man in his early thirties who wants to become financially free after having worked a 9-5 job for the past several years. After hearing a talk online about how eCommerce is the next big thing, John pours all of his time energy, and resources into creating a successful eCommerce store. After years of working, John has barely been able to make back his initial investments and finds himself in a rut, no matter what he does his stores never produce enough to sustain him.

So, what should John do in this situation: give up and go back to focusing on his day job or don't give up and continue to plow forward? The answer is neither. John should instead give up on the vehicle he is using to try and obtain his actual goal, financial freedom, while strongly holding on to the said goal. Perhaps John does not have the natural inkling to know what products consumers like to buy online, or perhaps he does not enjoy marketing, which is a huge aspect of eCommerce.

Either way, there may be other ventures that are better suited for John that will allow him to become financially free, not just eCommerce. Far too many people stick with a successful vehicle they are not suited to because they heard that it worked for other people, and also heard that they should never give up. However, if you are to become successful then you will need to find which vehicle works for you rather than choosing one that someone else chose. Only then will you be able to truly understand, appreciate, and experientially comprehend, the never-give-up attitude.

How Do I Change My Attitude?

The simple answer to this question is honesty. Without being honest about your current attitudes it will be almost impossible for anyone to change them.

However, being honest with yourself may not be that easy. As humans, we often become defensive when it comes to our belief systems, especially if we feel that they are not working for us. Our tendency is to double down on them because of pride. And as our experience tells us, if we would only take the time to listen, nothing could take us further from success.

Take some time alone each day to sit down quietly and think about your attitudes towards the most important things in life such as your relationships, your finances, your goals and aspirations, others in general, and yourself, as well as any area of life that you are involved in. Try to determine if your attitude is helpful or not when it comes to achieving what you want to achieve in each of those areas. Asking yourself basic questions such as "is this serving me?", "is this behavior hindering my success in any way, if so, how?" and "how can I alter my behavior and responses?" will allow you to be honest and truly discover your current attitudes and if they are in need of change. Once you have identified the attitudes that require modification you will have to actively remind yourself of the attitude you want to adopt instead.

However, this cannot be done with generalizations, but instead requires specificity. For example, if you find that you have a poverty mindset when it comes to finances you will not just be able to fix it by saying to yourself 'I believe in a prosperity mindset'. Instead, it would be more helpful to say to yourself, 'I will not buy any new video games with my next paycheck and instead use that money to invest in marketing classes'. Or similar. The reason this is a more effective strategy is that it provides specific action points. Without steps that can be acted upon right away, it will be difficult to solidify your new belief system due to the old habits and patterns, that were used to affirm the old attitude. Therefore, pay attention to how you act immediately after deciding you want to adopt a new attitude.

The Positive Attitude

A positive attitude can go a long way in life. However, it is not quite as easy to adopt as one may first hope... Cultivating a truly positive attitude, one that brings about success and long-lasting happiness is a journey like any other. And it also does not mean just blindly laughing and smiling at the misfortunes in life. This section will show you exactly what a positive attitude is, how to obtain it, how to use it, and how to share it.

Positive vs Negative Attitudes

Attitudes are often categorized into two simple sections: positive and negative attitudes. However, what can often become lost in this oversimplification is what the difference between the two actually is and how one can tell one from the other. In its most simple terms, a positive attitude is one that attempts to incorporate values, beliefs, and viewpoints that have a beneficial impact on either the person holding those, while a negative attitude is a set of values and beliefs that have or predict a detrimental outcome for the person holding them or for those around them.

For example, take Tim and Tom. Both men witness the same skydiving video online. Tim mentions how exciting it must be to experience that level of adrenaline and states that the freedom of someone who is skydiving must experience. He projects a positive life-enhancing experience in image form to both himself and those around him. Tom on the other hand mentions that sometimes parachutes fail to deploy and that backup parachutes are not devoid of malfunctions or entanglements. Of course, Tom is projecting negative imagery and experiences to both himself and those around him. While both statements by the two men are technically true, Tim has adopted a positive attitude towards the video while Tom has adopted a negative one.

Tim believes that the experience would be emotionally enriching for the person skydiving while Tom believes that it is likely to end in that person's death or severe injury. MindTools (2020) talks about positive and negative attitudes as being self-fulfilling prophecies. Because you have a certain viewpoint, to begin with, you may take micro-actions that will bring about the result that you believed would occur. Because of this reality, it is important to know to adopt positive attitudes over negative ones whenever possible because I believe it's true that what you focus on you get more of, whether that's positive or negative experiences.

How To Cultivate a Positive Attitude?

As stated above, obtaining a positive attitude is not something that happens in a single day. It takes years of focused effort and practice in order to truly internalize a positive attitude. However, just like with any other skill, with enough practice, you can become really good at it. When our brains attempt to learn new information, they create what is known as neural pathways, which are the electrical highways within our brain that represent certain physical actions and behaviors. By repeating something long enough, we strengthen those neural pathways and it becomes easier for us to access them (Forbes, 2014). This is how an Olympic swimmer is better and faster than someone who just swims once a week for fun, because of their extensive practice and more importantly, focus.

The same is true for a positive attitude. Simply put, you can obtain a positive attitude by following the simple steps below:

1. Notice The Silver Lining

The next time you are thrown into an uncomfortable situation, or one that would usually cause you frustration or anger, attempt to locate the silver lining within the incident. No matter how bad a situation may be, there are always some positives that can be taken from it. Get injured at the gym? You can spend the extra time connecting with your family. Get yelled at by your boss? Maybe it is a sign that you should move to that other company that has shown interest in you. Unfortunately, no one can help you and hold your hand to identify every single positive thing in a given situation, and it wouldn't be helpful. This is part of the skill we talked about previously and needs to be practiced from your own will.

2. Acknowledge The Bad

It is not helpful if you simply start to pretend that bad things do not happen. In fact, Simply Psychology (2019) has a definition for that: denial. Denial will not allow you to truly develop a positive attitude as not dealing with the bad aspects of a situation, through acknowledgment, acceptance, and planning for damage control will cause you subconscious stress which, if ignored long enough, will act itself out in negative behaviors and feelings which will be detrimental to your ability to cultivate a positive attitude.

3. Positive Network and Repetition

As mentioned before, you will have to practice this skill continuously over the next few years in order to intrinsically become a positive person. It can also help your development if you surround yourself with people who are either attempting, like yourself, to become more positive, as well as people who have already achieved that goal or are just naturally positive. This social feedback network will allow your brain to learn quicker and strengthen those neural pathways we mentioned earlier. And do not beat yourself up if you do not practice perfectly, things will look a bit messy at the beginning. However, over the months you will start to see your negative attitude drop off more naturally as your positive attitude takes over.

Also, make sure to eliminate people from your social network that do not embody the positive attitude you are trying to develop. Attitudes are like illnesses; they are infectious and spread from one person to another. Therefore, it is vital to manage your social network like a delicate ecosystem that needs all of the good and little of the bad.

Encouraging A Positive Attitude in Others

It is not easy to help someone to change. However, we all have loved ones, or know people that we would like to help and in order to help those around us, it is vital that we first help ourselves. By following the steps mentioned above you will be able to cultivate a positive attitude that lasts. It is important that you do not try to help someone else too early in your own journey, as their negative attitude may weigh you down and make progress difficult. However, later on, it is a noble thing to share what you have learned with others and to lead by example so to speak.

You can directly tell them about the steps that you took in order to become more positive. However, most people want to see results before they actually embark on any journey. So, therefore, the best thing that you can do for the people in your life is to show them how much happier and more successful you are. Naturally, they will begin to question how you did it, and this will allow you to share with them the secret of a positive attitude. However, it is important to remember that not everyone wants to change.

Do not try and waste your energy on people who show no real interest in your happiness or success, or who never express a genuine desire to see a change in their lives. Many people are happy being unhappy and it is not your job to fix them. Let people come to you because those that do are far more likely to truly make a lasting change in their own lives.

"We can't help everyone, but everyone can help someone" - Ronald Regan

Positive Thinking and Daily Routines

Unfortunately, just as is the case with many inherent truths, positive thinking has become somewhat of a buzz-phrase to use for social media addicts. However, there is a true power in positive thinking that needs and should be tapped by those who want to become truly successful. According to the Cleveland Clinic (2017) the average person has around 60,000 separate thoughts each day and the majority of those thoughts are negatively repeating ones. How would you feel if you had someone who follows you around everywhere you go when you try to eat, work or sleep and just constantly tells you about negative things? Surely, you would do your best to get rid of that person.

However, seeing as that person is your own mind, it is impossible to get rid of, nor should you want to. Instead, you should take that person from enemy to ally and train them to constantly tell you positive things. Now, these do not need to be empty or vain encouragements, but instead, be genuine positive thoughts that will be helpful to your everyday life. The key to controlling this is by becoming mindful of your own negative thoughts life. If you spot a negative thought in your mind pay close attention to it. Feel the negative emotion associated with it and then try to see whichever situation it is talking about in a more objective way. Analyze it and see if it can be viewed in a more positive light. By doing this enough you will be able to more easily eliminate a great number of your negative thoughts, allowing you to become much more emotionally healthy and mature. In addition to adopting a healthy thought life, there are other measures that you can take, day by day, which will allow you to adopt a more positive attitude.

1. Begin The Day Right

It is easy to let your mind wander to all the things that need to be done or the worries that just naturally float to the surface first thing in the morning. However, it is important that you get the first part of the day right. The military knows this, which is why they make their recruits meticulously make their bed right after waking up, as it allows them to cultivate an attitude of discipline and hard work. Therefore, if you want a positive attitude begin your day by reminding yourself of all the good things that may have happened the previous day. They may be absolutely tiny, such as having eaten a good meal for dinner, however, just acknowledging the joy you felt while experiencing that positive thing will allow you to create a better start to your day. In short, try to cultivate an optimistic and positive outlook on the day ahead by giving those positive thoughts just a little attention at the beginning of your day. That way you set yourself up for a successful day and eventually, a successful life.

2. Limit Social Media Viewing

There are several reasons why you should not spend too much time browsing through social media. However, the biggest reason is that it has, in many cases, become a place full of negativity. Whether it is your old school friend complaining about his drive to work or a news article talking about how the world will end in a year because of climate change, there is not a lot of positivity being spread around the average person's social media account. According to The Independent (2019), regular use of social networks such as Facebook has been shown to have a negative impact on a person's mental wellbeing. Therefore, either cut your social media time completely or try to only follow pages/people who do not engage in sharing negativity.

3. Become More Healthy

Your mind and body are not two separate entities with no correlations between them. More and more research is showing how being unhealthy can negatively impact your mental health, and therefore make it more difficult to adopt a positive attitude.

One of the simplest things you can do to improve your health is to drink more water. Studies have shown that at least 75% of Americans are chronically dehydrated. This could be because they get the majority of their fluid intake from soda and do not drink enough water.

So just add a bottle or two of plain water to your routine each day and see your health increase. This can then be coupled with light exercises, such as jogging or playing baseball, as well as eating more leafy greens, as many people are also mineral deficient. By addressing these things, and being disciplined day by day, it will become far easier for you to adopt a positive attitude.

Facing Your Fears

Undoubtedly in your pursuit of a positive attitude, you will run into a part of your internal life that most would rather ignore: your fears. Fears can be rational or irrational as people have phobias from everything including vicious dogs, water, and speaking in front of people, the list is endless. However, fear is a severely negative emotion, and if undealt with it can begin to take hold in your life and dictate all of your decisions. Just think back to the last week or month, there was likely an instance where you wanted to do something but didn't because of fear.

While there is no way to simply get rid of fears, the best thing that you can do is to face them head-on. By exposing yourself to the situation or thing that causes you to fear you will naturally create an adaptive response to that stimulus. It may be terrible at first and you may even want to run away and scream. However, if you are able to stick with it long enough then you may just find that your fear slowly stops having control over you and you will begin to regain control over it. Just remember that this is not a one-time process and exposure to the fear trigger needs to happen repeatedly for the therapy to work. If your phobia is severe, you can also consult an expert therapist as they will guide you through the process. However, when seeking to attain a positive attitude, you must at some point face and conquer your fears no matter what method you use.

Attitude Begins with Self-Awareness

A lot of things have been covered in this section and the information may be a little bit overwhelming. However, what is most important is to remember that your change in attitude begins with developing self-awareness. Most people suffer from intrinsic ignorance about their own beliefs, behaviors, emotions, etc., and it is that ignorance that stops them from truly taking control of their life. If someone develops a mindful attitude towards themselves before anything else, it will be far easier for that person to deal with everything else. After all, it is difficult to clean a house with your eyes closed, so why should it be easy to clean your mind without truly looking at it? Anyways, remember that attitude begins with self-awareness. Focus on yourself so you can begin to change yourself and what you may ultimately see as being negative about yourself and your life, and then get your attitude on your side working for you instead of against you.

PART 2:
Getting Your Attitude on Your Side

Make Your Attitude Your Very Best Friend!

In every aspect of your life, your attitude plays a big role. If you want to get ahead and be content in your life, then you have to get your attitude on your side.

Your attitude reflects in everything you do and everything that happens to you. What is referred to as The Law of Attraction is the concept that whatever you put out comes back to you. This is the whole idea of getting your attitude on your side.

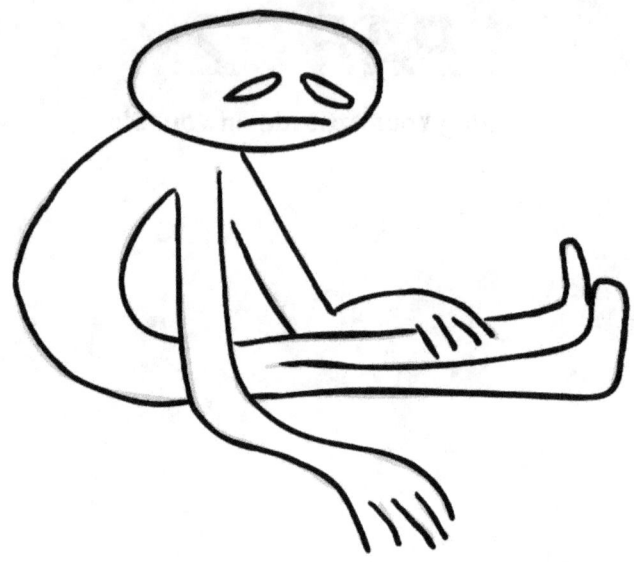

In order to get your attitude on your side, you have to learn what that means. You have to learn how to make your attitude positive and how to implement the idea of getting your attitude on your side in your life. And we covered some of those steps in part 1, however, we will dig just a little deeper and take a look from a different perspective in part 2.

It is going to take some work in order to be able to get your attitude on your side, but it is well worth it. As you will learn your attitude can paint your whole life and you can change everything about your current situation just by letting your attitude guide you.

What Does It Mean to Get Your Attitude on Your Side?

When you figuratively look at the idea of getting your attitude on your side, what you see is that it basically means the attitude you display is going to reflect in the path you take in life. In other words, your attitude will affect your life areas and it will help in determining what happens to you as a result.

Let us break it down and look at what 'getting your attitude on your side' really means in simple terms.

First, you have to define what "on your side" is. It is basically a path you travel down. It is befriending yourself in such a way that how you behave and act works positively for you. Your outcomes are positively affected by your attitude. Your attitude is the way you act, think, and treat those around you. Your attitude affects absolutely everything in your life. It greatly affects the way you think as well as behave and the effect of that is how others then treat you.

Now, to get your attitude on your side would mean to let your attitude guide you. Your attitude is going to shape everything in your life. You are going to be traveling down the path which your attitude leads you but of course, your attitude is first created or chosen by yourself.

So, the best thing to do is to adopt a positive attitude so that your "new friend" (your attitude!) takes you down a positive path. You have to choose to adopt a positive attitude in order to get it on your side.

Making your attitude your friend is about choosing what that friend is going to be. It is a personal act of creation. Is it going to be negative or positive? Is it going to be about hard work or laziness? And so on. The attitudes you choose to have in each area of your life is going to influence everything that happens during your life, so you should choose that friend wisely.

It is a common understanding that your attitude mold's or shapes many aspects of your life. Many people believe that a positive attitude brings about positive things, while a negative attitude brings negativity, and negative situations.

A good, healthy, positive attitude has a way of even influencing your environment, but it may not be in the way you think. Just because you have this positive attitude does not mean that everything will automatically go your way.

When you think positively you will be less likely to see the negative in things and therefore your environment will appear to change.

You will probably start to notice the little things more than ever before and that will have a good effect on you. In effect, you are creating your own environment by first adjusting your attitude to reflect that environment.

You will then be able to start believing in yourself more and to believe that you can accomplish anything if you put your mind to it. You will be able to set goals and reach them because you will believe that you can do it. You will not have that old, outworn, negative energy to hold you back.

As already suggested, a positive attitude is very influential. It will start to shape everyone and everything around you. You are going to see the great power it has almost immediately. The power of a positive attitude is anything but subtle. But of course, much bigger changes in your personal life will take time.

With this in mind, you have to decide what it is you want from life. Do you want positive experiences or negative experiences? That is really a silly question because most people are going to quickly say they want positive experiences, of course. We have created a whole program about creating a Better Life Experience that you will find at the back of this book but this title is about the way your attitude colors and affects that life experience.

People in general deal better with positive experiences than they do with negative experiences. People want to have a happy life without problems. They want a life that seems to just flow without roadblocks and challenges around every corner. Of course, most people are going to choose a positive path for their life rather than a negative one and so you should realize from the start that you create the life you experience for yourself.

No one else can do that for you, although some will try to influence you in one direction or another for their own benefit. It is up to you to make sure that you choose only what is good for you and the Better Life Experience you are creating for yourself and your loved ones.

In order to have good, positive things happen for you, you need to be very conscious of the fact that you are making your positive attitude your very best friend. You have to conduct yourself in positive ways, think about positive things, and live in a positive manner - you have to make your attitude your closest friend and ally which requires that you keep your thoughts of possessing a great attitude close to you by focusing on yourself, your thoughts and actions.

Different Ways to Get Your Attitude on Your Side

In order to get the influence of **a Positive Attitude,** you have to first learn how to get your attitude working for you and not against you. So just how do you get your attitude on your side?

It is all about believing in the idea that your attitude affects your life and what happens to you as a consequence. If you struggle with believing that if you think positively that positive things will happen, then the first step in making your attitude your ally is to change your way of thinking.

You have to believe in the idea that a positive attitude equals positive results, and these will be subtle to begin with and build over time. You have to start looking for proof of that fact. It should not be hard to find since positive influence is all around. And, if you cannot find the proof you need, just take a good look at what is happening around you because you will come to realize that it is you yourself that creates those positive results in your life, through your actions and behaviors.

Try it out for yourself. There is no better proof than seeing it firsthand as you create it. Take one day and commit to having a positive attitude all day. Take notice of how others react to you.

Are they friendlier? Do people seem to help you out more than usual? What other things happen during the day? Can you see the positive attitude influencing other things in your life during the day?

Once you have convinced yourself that your positive attitude really does influence your life, then you can begin to put the idea of making your attitude your very best friend and ally into play.

As you can no doubt see, this is an act of creation on your part. It is cause and effect in motion and under your control.

Keep up the positive attitude, let it influence your life and then let it lead you to good things. Eventually, it will, although, in the beginning, the results may be subtle but stretched out into your future the results can be and often are massive. You will start to see how it brings good things to you almost instantly but be patient and you will see bigger results as you progress down the path with your new best friend.

Making your attitude your friend should incorporate your ideas, the way you think, your actions and body language, and even your goals.

You have to make an effort to start turning all your thoughts and ideas into positive thoughts and ideas believing that you cannot fail. You have to start pushing the negativity out of your head and let positive thoughts guide you.

Every time you start to find your thoughts drifting towards the negative, you have to make a conscious effort to make them positive instead. It helps to train yourself to always find the positive in anything. If you train your thoughts to turn to the positive it will go a long way towards changing your attitude.

You just think the opposite of the negative thoughts and ideas.

Instead of thinking "I can't do that", think instead," This will be challenging but I can and will do it". And then reaffirm this often.

Your Body Language says a lot about you too. Body language can tell others all about your attitude and personality. That is why it is incredibly important to make sure your body language is positive and confident. And remember that confidence is a choice.

Body language is, of course, the movements of your body, the way you hold your body, and your facial expressions, including eye movement. Body language often corresponds with our attitudes and sometimes contradicts what our words are saying.

When our body language and our words do not match, people are likely to believe the body language as it is often an unconscious thing that gives away the truth about who you are being.

Positive body language is when your body is open. You do not want to do things that close your body off, like crossing your arms. You want to make eye contact and face people when talking to them openly.

A smile is the best body language you can display to others. Keeping a smile on your face will also benefit your attitude. Smiles have a way of making you feel good, so always be sure to have a smile on your face. It's easier and takes less energy than frowning. Smiling is giving to yourself as well as to those around you.

Goals are important in any aspect of your life. Goals can help you make things happen. Setting positive goals and sticking to them will help you maintain your positive attitude as well as build your confidence as you achieve the smaller goals on your way to the big ones.

By maintaining your positive attitude and letting it lead you to good experiences, you are indeed making your attitude your very best friend and ally.

Definition of a Positive Attitude

Just to put it out there in clear terms, here is a checklist of what a positive attitude is and what it looks like and involves.

Use this checklist to make sure your attitude is 100% positive. A positive person will have the following characteristics:

- Upbeat and cheerful.
- Looks at the glass as half full not half empty.
- It can help you to find the beauty in anything.
- Think of the good before the bad.
- Loves life.
- Avoids negative words.
- Loves to have fun.
- Never puts others down.
- Genuinely cares about those around him/her.
- It looks for ways to make others' lives better too.
- Is a giver, not a taker?
- It does not hurt others.
- It can help you to see the solution over the problem.
- Willing to work towards goals.

Do the things on this checklist seem like you or are they the opposite of how you really act? If you really want to be a positive person, you will align yourself with this checklist and in some cases practice each or at least keep them close to your heart and mind. You will strive to become everything here and to become a person that can honestly say this list describes them perfectly.

There are many ways you can begin to shape yourself into a positive person. Take some or all of these tips and put them to use in your life and become that positive person you strive to be.

Positive Living Tips

It is rather simple to separate the positive from the negative.

However, it can be quite difficult to stop yourself from running to the negative. This is simply human nature. It is something we are programmed to do. Do not feel bad about this natural inclination.

Instead, choose to do something about it.

Here are some tips for adding some positive influence to your life:

Find a happy place. Create a place in your mind that is your ideal paradise. When you feel stressed or down just go to your happy place, relax there and enjoy it.

Get a hobby. Do something you enjoy that will raise your spirits and allow you to maintain a positive attitude.

Exercise. While many people look at exercise in a negative way, it really can bring positive influences to your life. The body's natural reaction to exercise is a good one. You will even begin to feel better and therefore act better if you adopt an exercise routine.

Find affirmations. Affirmations are sayings, verses, or other short phrases that can have a positive influence on you. Affirmations can be a quote, a verse from the Bible, or even a line from a greeting card. They are simply words, or phrases, or something else that makes you think positively or even just bring a smile to your face. Reverse version of your negative thoughts are also great to use such as the one given earlier.

Using an affirmation daily can perk up your attitude in an instant.

Exploring new things. Instead of walking away from what is unknown, walk towards it and give it a try.

Do not walk away from a challenge. Let yourself accept the many challenges you will meet and try creative ways to deal with them.

Make a mess. Make messes to learn from them. Do not get caught up in caring about the mess you create. Happiness can be messy at times and unrestricted.

Ignore the rules. You can end up having a fun time simply because you are doing something you were specifically told not to do.

Defying authority can be an adrenaline rush. Break a few rules now and then. But of course, be cautious and don't put yourself or others in any danger.

Pretend. Imagination is a wonderful thing. Allow yourself to go to some make-believe place. Get away from your normal life and pretend you are someone else. Have fun and you are sure to smile at the very least. You could also imagine yourself as someone who has all the great qualities that you yourself seek.

You can take these tips and build upon them. You can surely come up with things that have a way of making you happy.

Only you know what makes you smile, so take that and run with it. Allow whatever it is that makes you happy to guide you to your new positive attitude and your Better Life Experience.

PART 3:
Your New Best Friend

Using Your Attitude as Your Best Friend

It may seem very easy to just get your attitude on your side working for you instead of against you, and you probably won't need a lot of convincing to at least give it a try. After all, what do you have to lose?

If you are focused on your attitude and have become used to letting it lead you through your life, then it is, or should be something you are already familiar with and so you may already know how you act, behave and move through life.

People make their attitude their best friend all the time. Most of the time they do it without even realizing it. Unfortunately, most of the time the attitude is a negative one, and of course... there is such a thing as negative friends too!

It is often easier to see how a negative attitude acts as a negative friend than how a positive attitude acts as a positive friend. This is just human nature to see negative over positive, due to our engrained flight or fight response system. We then become focused on living in lack so the positive things are not given the attention and gratitude they deserve. Pessimistic attitudes seem to flood the world, while at the same time optimism is slowly drowning. Or at least as been until now, as you become more focused on how your attitudes affect the results you get in life.

You can probably come up with many examples of how negative thinking or a negative attitude has turned into a somewhat negative situation. You can probably point out negative people and give plenty of examples of how their negative attitude is influencing their own life.

You may even be able to look at your own life and see how negativity has affected you. It's likely you have let a negative attitude direct you in at least one situation or area in your life.

Can you remember a time when your negative attitude caused problems in a particular situation? You can probably look at it now and see just how the negative attitude worked against you. Even if the situation was not a positive one to begin with, your negative attitude most likely comes into play at some point in the process.

While this can begin to show you how an attitude adjustment can help to become your ally, it should also teach you that you should want to do everything possible to make absolutely sure that your attitude is a positive and helpful one on a continuing basis.

If you really want to get your attitude on your side and you want that friend to be a positive one, then you need to start looking at the positive things in your life and recognize them as such. You have to train your mind to find the positive in everything and then show a little gratitude for it.

You have to ignore the negatives and then take the negatives you cannot ignore and turn them into positives through positive action. I mean, just imagine your friend filled with negativity and there are roadblocks and other things that get in your way or cause you to not be able to walk the path you choose. You may at some point, have to work and inject a little effort in order to get around these negative obstacles and situations.

If your friend is positive, then it is filled with positive feelings and outlooks. There are then no roadblocks that you cannot handle. Anything that stands in your way is then easy to get past and dealt with more quickly.

You can clearly see that a positive attitude is much better than a negative attitude. You would, obviously, rather have a friend that is easy to get along with than one filled with issues, negative situations, and things that get in your way and slow you down.

Using your attitude as your best friend involves many levels of changing your life. You will have to change things you do daily, through your interactions with other people, your thoughts, and your goals in order to see positive results.

And as already mentioned, the way you shape your thoughts and goals will go a long way towards helping you shape your attitude and making your attitude your new best friend. So, make sure you make a conscious effort to keep these things in check.

When you interact with other people in your life you are basically broadcasting your attitude to them. You want this to always be good and positive so that people react to you in a positive manner, if as suggested, you approach them in a positive manner. Your interaction with others is very important in your life. You can surely see the CAUSE and EFFECT of this. Positive causes equal positive effects.

You want those interactions to be positive because it will allow you to bring positive things into your life more easily. A good example is during a job interview. If you approach the interview with a negative and sloppy attitude, then you likely will not get the job because the employer is most likely positive and will want to be around positive people. His business depends on it.

Go to the same interview with a positive attitude and you have a better chance of getting that job. The way you approach others can have a huge impact on your life, so make sure you are using your attitude as your best friend when interacting with others.

Your attitude should be your closest friend every single day and every moment of every day in everything that you say or do. It will take some time to make it a regular routine but it can be done over a relatively short period with a little attention and focus.

In the beginning, you will likely have to work hard to find the areas in your life where you lack a great attitude and to make sure you are being positive in every aspect of your life.

You will have to make an effort to stay positive and to think positively. It can be difficult, especially if you often give in to negative thoughts and actions which again calls for being positive and remaining positive until you succeed. Self-discipline is key.

It is also common when you approach a situation in a positive manner that you end up having a positive experience. People are more likely to help you and to go out of their way to make sure you get what you need when you approach things in a positive manner, in the present as well as into the future. So, with your attitude as your friend, you are opening yourself up to a lot of positive experiences and New Friends. Positive ones.

Using your attitude as your best friend is about making everything in your life positive and possible. That means associating with positive people, keeping yourself in good wholesome, positive situations, and surrounding yourself with positive people and things.

You have to get rid of negativity all together in every corner of your life and being. You have to start and then continue being positive about everything. By doing this, you are continuously choosing or creating your own best friend in your attitude. You are paving your road through the mire of life's negative situations with positive energy and this will lead you to positive results.

What Making Your Attitude Your Friend Can Do for You?

Once you start to live with the idea of making your attitude your very best friend you will start to see changes, especially if you have been living with a negative attitude and have decided to change it to a more positive one.

Adopting a positive attitude and making it your close friend as you travel through life will impact your life in many ways. You are going to start to see the positive effects and influence more or less immediately.

People are going to start treating you in a more positive manner. People respond positively to someone who greets them with a positive attitude. I am sure you have experienced this before. Think of a time when you gave a stranger a smile. They most likely smiled back, didn't they? That is a positive attitude at work.

Sometimes it will not be that clear cut. You will also be using your attitude to influence people in other ways, too. As you start to adapt your positive attitude to your life, you will begin to see the positive in everything especially in the way that people respond and react to you.

No matter what happens to you in your life, your positive attitude will help you through it with more pride and dignity than before.

You will find a way to overcome almost anything without getting mad, upset, or depressed about it. Basically, you will learn how to look at life very differently and not just with a more positive outlook, but with knowing that your positive outlook is creating a Better Life Experience. I strongly believe that we choose state as we move through life.

You will be able to approach problems and difficult situations better. You will be able to handle adversity better. You will be able to overcome things that before would have dragged you down.

Making your attitude your friend may go even deeper than you could ever have imagined. If you suffer from an addiction, like smoking cigarettes, or worse, you may be able to quit once and for all just by making your attitude your friend, simply because you gain more respect for yourself.

Think about why you smoke or indulge in damaging addictions or habits. Many people give reasons such as they smoke to deal with stress, to calm themselves down, to relax. If you have a reason like this, then you will no longer need to smoke once you get your attitude on your side, or at the very least stopping the bad habit could be made much easier.

This is because you will be able to handle stress on your own without outside help. You will also be less likely to experience situations that you feel you cannot handle. You will no longer reach for addictions, like cigarettes, to help you through stress because your attitude will be guiding you instead.

Quitting your smoking or other habit will become something that you will feel you can do relatively easy because you will not feel that strong psychological need for a cigarette anymore. It is quite possible to help yourself through a hard habit, such as smoking, with your new positive attitude.

Making your attitude your friend will literally transform your life. You are going to be projecting a positive vibe and it will come back to you. You will start to see how positive things happen in your life. You will begin to draw positive influences to you. You will become a magnet for positive experiences. It will almost seem strange how much your new positive attitude affects your life.

You can look at making your attitude your very best friend in many different ways. It really depends upon your personal ideas and thoughts. Some people may believe that it is along the lines of karma and what you send out will come back to you. Others may believe it is the law of attraction at work or simply a mental thing, where you think positive and therefore you see positive.

No matter what your opinion is on how a positive attitude works in your life, the bottom line is that making your attitude your ally is a winning idea and a great move to make. You cannot deny the power of making your attitude your ally once you first start implementing it in your life. You will soon see that for yourself.

In my own personal view attitude is a cause. It is this cause that affects your life in different ways. Positive causes such as being positive, appreciative, kind, friendly all produce positive effects.

Some call this the law of attraction as I said, but I like to keep things simple and so making positive causes is more practical for me and I see the positive effects almost immediately in most cases.

An Example of Making Your Attitude Your Friend

It can be quite easy for someone to just tell you that making your attitude your ally is a good idea. However, until you actually see it at work, you may not fully believe in the idea itself. Here is a story about how making your attitude your friend can work beautifully. How it can help transform a lousy life into something great.

Janet was quite a pessimistic person. She approached every situation thinking the worst would happen. She never tried to even think about the positives within those situations. Janet rarely smiled and she often spoke very negatively about everyone and everything in her life.

Janet had high blood pressure, no close friends, a job she hated and she was deep in debt. She read an article about how making your attitude your friend will help guide you in life and how that attitude needs to be positive if you want a happy, productive, and positive life.

Janet considered what she had read and decided to put the idea to work for her. She figured she had nothing to lose.

The next morning when she woke up, the same negative thoughts began creeping into her mind. Instead of embracing them as she usually did, she pushed them away and replaced them with positive thoughts. She wrote here new positive affirmations and began to repeat them throughout the day to give her self a boost.

Instead of anticipating the traffic jam she usually encountered on the way to work, she thought only about her favorite song playing on the radio and thought about how lucky she was to be able to hear it that particular morning.

When she reached her office, instead of simply rushing into her office as she usually did, she smiled at a few co-workers and stopped to have a chat with the secretary. She was effectively telling everyone in here office how much she had changed.

She started to do her job as well as she could, and her boss even acknowledged her good work on the project she had just completed when he came in. She noted that if she had rushed to her office, she would not have even been standing there for him to talk to.

Later that day her boss called her into his office. He talked to her about how she seemed different today. He said he was glad to see her that morning because it reminded him of what a good worker she is and he had realized she was perfect for the opening in management that he needed to fill.

Janet ended up getting a promotion.

After that day Janet kept making her attitude her best friend. She trained herself to be positive and things started to really look up in her life. She made some friends at work and she started to feel better about herself and her life.

When Janet turned her attitude into a positive one and made her attitude her best friend, she started to live a life she could only long for before. Her life began to reflect here new positive thoughts.

The same thing could happen to you. Get your attitude on your side and see how it works out for you. Just like Janet, a simple chance meeting created due to your attitude change could change your life too?

Why did this work for Janet? Take a constructive look at her situation.

Janet usually sat in traffic and fumed about how it was slowing her down. She went straight to the negative and even though her favorite song had probably played on the radio during her morning commute, she was so stuck in the negative that she never even noticed it before.

Today, Janet was open to hearing the song and actually enjoying hearing it, and so, when she did hear it, she got a slight boost in the way she felt. Joyful songs can pick you up and make you feel better. It was that slight boost that helped her to remain calm and relaxed while sitting in traffic.

Besides the immediate effect of Janet feeling calmer and being able to handle her traffic jam, there is also the fact that calming down and letting go of the stress is good for her health. Her blood pressure and pulse were likely lower than normal and that is great for her heart health. Sometimes accepting a problem such as a traffic jam can be much easier and healthier to handle than going off on one so to speak.

Janet never greeted anyone in her office with any positive emotions. She just went to her office every morning and sat by herself. Today, she actually took the time to smile at co-workers and even talk. She was able to start building relationships at the office which will help her to be happier about going to work and subsequently enjoy the office much more.

Having her boss come in while she was socializing gave her some much-needed face time with him. Had she not been out there he would have never even considered her for the promotion.

Janet made many changes in her life just in one day. Imagine what could happen over a much longer period of time and more importantly, what could happen for you too. Could making such changes impact your life in a big way too?

Yes, it absolutely can. So, you have nothing to lose by allowing yourself to try making your attitude your best friend.

Summing It Up

Now that you have learned what making your attitude your friend means and how to implement the idea in your life, you can clearly see it is an idea worth putting to the test.

Through the ideas presented here, you should be able to get started making your attitude your friend with no bother at all. You should find that changing your attitude to a positive one is quite simple. The initial practical steps were given in art 1 and some additional possibilities resented in parts 2 and 3.

Once you put your mind to it, and make a list of the changes you are going to make to yourself, your attitude and your life, there is nothing stopping you from reaping the rich rewards of having a positive attitude and better life experience simply by taking full advantage of the Attitude Advantage and reaping the positive effects of it.

It is all about taking that first step.

You have to decide to be committed to the process. You have to commit to becoming a positive person. You have to set a goal to become a positive person and let that positive attitude lead you.

Goals are very powerful. They can drive you and help you to accomplish things you never thought possible until you made a comprehensive list and one by one eliminated them by achieving them. When you have a set of goals you work harder and you feel as if you have to accomplish them. Set your goal to make your attitude positive and to make your new positive attitude your very best friend.

Remember what making your attitude your friend can do:

- It can help you to look at life in a positive way.

- It can allow you to see challenges and adversity in a new light that you are much more able to handle, easily.

- It can help reduce stress, which helps you remain healthy for longer, so ar able to inject more positive effort into your goals and life in general.

- It can also help you influence others to live in a positive manner, so will increase your popularity with friends.

- It can make you a new person who sees and achieves more in life.

- It can allow you to begin to love life like never before.

Keep Janet's story in your mind and let it help you to create your own positive changes and help you to stay committed towards your new positive attitude. Let the examples from her story remind you that good can come from all of this work and even from small changes you make in your life.

- You have learned what making your attitude your best friend means.

- You know that by projecting a positive attitude you will reap positive rewards.

- You learned what exactly a positive attitude is and how you can start to make your attitude positive.

You are now armed with loads of basic information on how to become a positive person and how to live a more positive life. The rest is in your hands. No one can force you into living positively. No one can make you to get the Attitude Advantage. However, after all you've learned, can you honestly say you would pass up the opportunity to make your life so much better?

Do you not want to see how great your life can be?

Are you sure you can live, knowing what you know now, without at least giving it a try?

Chances are you are now so excited about the possibilities that a positive attitude is all you'll think about over the next few days. Subconsciously you will start to change and by then, it will be too late to even consider ignoring all you've learned and the changes you made without even noticing.

You will be on your way to making your attitude your friend without even putting up much effort. You will surely start to reap the rewards. But why wait? Making your attitude your friend is something that you can begin doing today, so what is holding you back?

Drop the negative thoughts. Put a smile on your face and start projecting your positive attitude to everyone. Take all the tips and advice you've read here and put them to use. And if you have to, fake it until you make it.

Get your attitude on your side. Change your life. Become a better person. Help those around you live a better life. Become a role model. Be everything you can be.

You have nothing to lose and everything to gain, so make your attitude positive and then even more positive. Then take your positive attitude and get your attitude on your side. Do it now and you will never want to go back to being a negative thinker again.

The key to a fulfilling life of wealth and success is in your hands, you just need to take advantage of the possibilities and start building even better results in your life. Either way... I wish you and your new best friend, all the success life has to offer...

Thanks for Listening

Andy Raingold

Did You Enjoy Reading Attitude Advantage?

I would like to thank you for purchasing and reading this book. I hope you enjoyed it and that it provided some value to yourself and your life.

If you enjoyed reading this book and found some benefit in it, I'd love your support and hope that you could take a moment to post a review at the store where you found this book. I'd love to hear from you, even if you have feedback, as it will help me in ensuring that I improve this book and others in the future.

Other Books by Andy Raingold

Attitude Advantage
Freedom from Addictions
Your Assertive Life
Attraction Master
Communication Master
Focused Concentration
Fast Learning Genius
Enhance Yourself and Your Life
Unlimited Energy
Set High Goals Then Reach Them
Reboot Your Metabolism
Mind Mapping Mastery Tips
Raise Your Personal Motivation
Easily Defeat & Dump Procrastination
Subconscious Programming
Tap into The Universe
Unleash Your Power
Creative Visualization
Your Perfect Memory
Your Unlimited Power
Strategies to Boost Productivity
How to Become an Effective Manifestor
Boost Your Self Esteem
Listen to Yourself

DISCOVER: A Simple Process That Moves You into Greater Success and Happiness and <u>The Life You Truly Want</u>. At the Same Time Developing A Deeper Understanding of Yourself, Your Life, and The Journey Ahead!

You Don't Have to Struggle Alone... You Can Now Go Through the Whole Upgrade Your Happiness Process Through the Online Interactive Workshop Edition!

Just visit www.upgradeyourhappiness.com/sl to find out more.

You can also get an additional 20% off the marked price when you use the discount coupon below:

20% DISCOUNT COUPON: UYH2021

DISCLAIMER AND TERMS OF USE AGREEMENT

The author and publisher have used their best efforts in preparing this report. The author and publisher make no representation or warranties with respect to the accuracy, applicability, fitness, or completeness of the contents of this report. The information contained in this report is strictly for educational purposes. Therefore, if you wish to apply the ideas contained in this report, you are taking full responsibility for your actions.

EVERY EFFORT HAS BEEN MADE TO ACCURATELY REPRESENT THIS PRODUCT AND Its POTENTIAL. HOWEVER, THERE IS NO GUARANTEE THAT YOU WILL IMPROVE IN ANY WAY USING THE TECHNIQUES AND IDEAS IN THESE MATERIALS. EXAMPLES IN THESE MATERIALS ARE NOT TO BE INTERPRETED AS A PROMISE OR GUARANTEE OF ANYTHING. SELF-HELP AND IMPROVEMENT POTENTIAL IS ENTIRELY DEPENDENT ON THE PERSON USING OUR PRODUCT, IDEAS, AND TECHNIQUES.

YOUR LEVEL OF IMPROVEMENT IN ATTAINING THE RESULTS CLAIMED IN OUR MATERIALS DEPENDS ON THE TIME YOU DEVOTE TO THE PROGRAM, IDEAS AND TECHNIQUES MENTIONED, KNOWLEDGE, AND VARIOUS SKILLS. SINCE THESE FACTORS DIFFER ACCORDING, TO INDIVIDUALS, WE CANNOT GUARANTEE YOUR SUCCESS OR IMPROVEMENT LEVEL. NOR ARE WE RESPONSIBLE FOR ANY OF YOUR ACTIONS.

MANY FACTORS WILL BE IMPORTANT IN DETERMINING YOUR ACTUAL RESULTS AND NO GUARANTEES ARE MADE THAT YOU WILL ACHIEVE RESULTS SIMILAR TO OURS OR ANYBODY ELSE'S, IN FACT, NO GUARANTEES ARE MADE THAT YOU WILL ACHIEVE ANY RESULTS FROM OUR IDEAS AND TECHNIQUES IN OUR MATERIAL.

The author and publisher disclaim any warranties (express or implied), merchantability, or fitness for any particular purpose. The author and publisher shall in no event be held liable to any party for any direct, indirect, punitive, special, incidental, or other consequential damages arising directly or indirectly from any use of this material, which is provided "as is", and without warranties.

As always, the advice of a competent professional should be sought.

The author and publisher do not warrant the performance, effectiveness, or applicability of any sites listed or linked to in this report. All links are for information purposes only and are not warranted for content, accuracy, or any other implied or explicit purpose.

You are encouraged to print this book for easy reading.